GOPAL
The Invincible

Adapted from the writings of
His Divine Grace
A.C. Bhaktivedanta Swami Prabhupada

Illustrations by Sunita devi dasi

Retold by Yogesvara dasa and Jyotirmayi devi dasi

Gopal the Invincible is based on the *Bhāgavata-purāna*, available in English under the title *Śrīmad-Bhāgavatam* (©1978 by the Bhaktivedanta Book Trust), translated from the original Sanskrit by His Divine Grace A.C. Bhaktivedanta Swami Prabhupāda, Founder-*Ācārya* of the International Society for Krishna Consciousness.

ꕗ

Library of Congress Cataloging in Publication Data

Yogeśvara Dāsa.
   Gopal the Invincible.

   (Classics from India for children)
   "Based on the Bhāgavatapurāna ... translated from the original Sanskrit by ... A.C. Bhaktivedanta Swami Prabhupāda"--Verso t.p.
   Summary: Krishna, known as Gopal the cowherd boy, proves himself a worthy match for the nefarious creatures who come to disturb the life of his peaceful forest village.
   1. Puranas. Bhāgavatapurāna--Paraphrases, English--Juvenile literature. [1. Krishna (Hindu deity)
2. Mythology, Hindu] I. Jyotirmayi-devī. II. Sunīta-devī, ill. III. Puranas. Bhāgavatapurāna. IV. Title.
V. Series.
BL1140.4.B435Y63 1982   294.5'211   82-16396
ISBN 0-89647-017-2

PRINTED IN ITALY
BY

EDITOR ℮

Long ago, in the north of present-day India, ruled the wicked king Kamsa. Fearful of the prophecy that he would one day be killed by the eighth son of his sister Devaki, Kamsa had decreed that every newborn child in his kingdom should be slain. At that time, Krishna, the Supreme Personality of Godhead, appeared as Devaki's eighth child, for it was His mission to defend the righteous and destroy evil-doers. To protect his child from Kamsa's wrath, Devaki's husband Vasudev carried Krishna across the sacred Yamuna River to the home of his brother Nanda, and their passage across the Yamuna was sheltered from the night's rain by the celestial serpent Ananta. There in Nanda's forest village of Gokul, Krishna was known as Gopal the cowherd boy.

In those days children received their astrological charts from an expert priest. Krishna and His elder brother Balaram received Theirs from the saintly brahmin Gargamuni.

"This beautiful child Krishna," Gargamuni told Nanda and his wife Yasoda, "has the spiritual qualities of the Supreme Personality of Godhead. He has appeared many times on earth in different forms to protect the pious and destroy evil doers. Now He has again come to fulfill that mission. Happiness and good fortune will be yours by His grace. He will offer protection from many dangers, but His childhood will be disturbed by the attacks of numerous demons. Raise Him and protect Him carefully."

Child Krishna sang and danced His way into the hearts of all the villagers. If asked, He would fetch His father's wooden shoes or some kitchen utensil, just like an ordinary child. He would carry out the order with great effort and strike His body with His arms to show how strong He was. If the object was too heavy, He would just stand there looking helpless.

Like most other children, Krishna and Balaram preferred to play with Their friends rather than return home for lunch. "Come," Mother Yasoda would call. "Your father is waiting for You to come eat. So dirty You are! Now take Your bath and put on fresh clothes. Later You may go back to play with the other boys."

Sometimes Krishna's pastimes revealed His divine nature. Once a woman selling fruit came to Nanda's house. Little Krishna took a handful of grains and ran to trade with her, just as He had seen His parents do. As He ran, most of the grains fell from His tiny palms.

"You want to trade these few grains for fruit?" the woman said. "That's all right. Take as much as You like." Then she filled Krishna's outstretched arms with plump, juicy fruits.

At once her basket overflowed with jewels and gold, for Krishna always appreciates the offerings of His devotees and rewards them millions of times over.

Life was not always so carefree for the residents of Gokula. King Kamsa feared his death at the hands of Krishna and sent powerful demons to attack the child. When Krishna was only a tiny baby, the witch Putana tried to kill Him. She smeared poison on her breast and then nursed the small child. Krishna drew out her life along with her milk, and Putana fell to the ground with a crash. Although she came in disguise, when she died her huge witch's form was revealed.

On a different occasion, an evil spirit crept inside a handcart and waited for a chance to harm baby Krishna. With His small foot Krishna kicked the cart, broke it to pieces, and the demon was crushed.

There was another attack when Krishna was one year old. This time a demon came in the shape of a gigantic whirlwind and carried the child off into the sky. Krishna made Himself heavier than a mountain and grabbed the demon by the throat. The whirlwind demon choked and fell lifeless to the ground, where his body smashed on a big slab of stone.

So many demons came to attack the child that Nanda's brother Upananda called a meeting of all the cowherd men. Something had to be done. Upananda addressed them with the wisdom of his years.

"By the Lord's mercy our dear Krishna remains unharmed despite the attacks of demons," he said. "But we must take care to protect Him from future dangers. I propose we leave Gokula and move our village to Vrindavan, where the groves overflow with fruits, flowers, and lush green grasses. Krishna will be safer there. If you agree, we can prepare our bullock carts this very day."

Without delay, the villagers packed their belongings on carts. Old men, women, and children rode on the carts, while the cows walked ahead. The cowherd men walked alongside the carts to protect the procession with their bows and arrows. As they travelled, the men blew their bugles and the women sang of Krishna's miraculous pastimes.

Soon they arrived at Vrindavan forest where life was pleasant in all seasons. By evening the cowherd men had arranged the carts in a semi-circle by thorny bushes as a temporary shelter, and soon they set about rebuilding their village.

In due course of time, Krishna and Balaram grew old enough to take care of the calves. Each day They set out for the pasturing grounds with Their friends and calves. The boys used ropes and stones to make fruits fall from the trees. The hard ones were especially good for playing ball. Sometimes the brothers covered Themselves with a blanket and mooed loudly, pretending to be a cow or a bull. Vrindavan had many animals such as peacocks, cuckoos, ducks, swans, monkeys, and frogs. The boys enjoyed imitating all these creatures and passed their days in great happiness.

Then, one day, demons again began their attacks. A strange new calf appeared in the herd. "That's the demon Vatsasura disguised as a calf," Krishna warned His elder brother. Quickly They sneaked up, and Krishna grabbed the demon's hind legs and tail. He twirled the imposter around and threw him into a tall fruit tree. As he fell, the demon's body expanded to a huge size and broke the tree, scattering fruits everywhere.

"Well done, Gopal!" cried the cowherd boys, gathering the sweet fruits from the ground. As usual at such happy moments, demigods showered victory flowers on Krishna from the heavenly planets.

What were the cowherd men to do? They had come to Vrindavan to find a safe place for Krishna to live. Yet killing demons was again becoming daily routine work for Him, as much as tending the calves.

One such encounter happened by the Yamuna River. The boys and calves were drinking water as usual after playing. Suddenly they saw a bird as big as a mountain peak. The bird, named Bakasura, swiftly lowered his sharp beak and swallowed Krishna with one gulp. The boys were frightened by the huge bird, but seeing him devour their beloved Krishna was more than they could bear and they nearly fainted with fear for His safety.

Krishna acted quickly and used His divine powers to become hot like fire and burn the demon's throat. In great pain, the giant bird threw Him up. Furious to see Krishna unharmed, the demon pounced again with his sharp beak. Krishna caught hold of the huge beak and split it apart as easily as a child might split a blade of grass.

The cowherd boys were amazed. With a great feeling of relief, they gathered around their friend and embraced Him with great delight. The boys rounded up their calves and returned home singing of Krishna's heroic pastimes. The cowherd men and women listened intently to the events of the day and received their children as though from the mouth of death.

"How extraordinary," the villagers thought. "This child seems practically invincible! Each time Krishna is attacked, He escapes unharmed and the evil-doer is destroyed. They have all perished like flies rushing into a fire. It is astonishing how the predictions of sage Gargamuni are all coming true!"

The villagers of Vrindavan never knew Krishna as the Supreme Personality of Godhead. For them He was simply their wonderful child Krishna, whose pastimes are so exciting to tell that they are worth telling another time, in another book.